PEASE PORRIDGE HOT

PEASE PORRIDGE HOT

*Recipes, Household Hints & Home
Remedies of the Pease Family*

Annotated by

KATHERINE HART

A WATERLOO BOOK *published by* THE ENCINO PRESS
For THE FRIENDS *of the* AUSTIN PUBLIC LIBRARY
1967

WATERLOO BOOK
Number 2

THIRD PRINTING

FOREWORD

AMONG THE MASS OF PAPERS given to the Austin-Travis County Collection of the Austin Public Library by the descendants of Elisha Marshall Pease, Governor of Texas, 1853-1857, there are many significant letters, both official and personal, written and received by this distinguished Texan and his family. The young Marshall Pease had come from Connecticut to settle in Texas in 1835. He started reading law in the office of Don Carlos Barrett at Mina (now Bastrop), and was soon involved in the growing movement to secure independence for Texas from Mexico. He fought in the first battle of the Texas Revolution, but ill health prevented him from continuing in the army. From 1835 on he acted in various capacities in different offices and on different committees of the emerging Texas government. Thus he began a long career of public service, during which he helped to shape the growth of Texas from a struggling colony to a prosperous state. Between his terms in public office, Pease engaged in an active law practice, first in Brazoria, then in Austin after 1857. As a private citizen and in his profession, his ability and integrity were generally recognized.

Governor Pease's wife, his children and grandchildren too made their contribution to the development and enrichment of the social and cultural life of their home city, Austin, and of the state of Texas as a whole. When the Governor-elect and his wife moved from Brazoria to Austin in 1853, the Republic of Texas was no more, and Austin had been the capital of one of the United States for eight years. Austin's growth from a frontier town into a capital city worthy of a great state involved many changes that were recorded by Mrs. Pease and her daughters in their prolific and observant correspondence. Their letters have value as social documents, quite apart from their relationship to Governor Pease's eminence.

Along with these more important letters and documents, there are in the Pease papers many reminders of the fact that the family, despite their political and social prominence, had to struggle, as do we all, with the common problems of daily existence. In 19th century Texas, there were no TV dinners, no ready cooked foods, and the feeding of the family was a matter of first concern to the mother. Also, there was an even greater shortage of doctors then than now, and the health of the family, and of the slaves, depended largely on the wisdom and attention of the master and mistress of the household in their practice as amateur physicians.

In the light of the literally hundreds of magazines and books devoted to the art of housekeeping today, these reminders of how a distinguished Texas family faced its own similar problems in the 19th century may prove interesting. Reading the home remedies in the light of today's medical knowledge can furnish amusement. The hand written recipes, which are reproduced here, though not numerous, are examples of the type of cookery the guest was offered at hospitable Woodlawn, the home of the Pease family and descendants for a century. Readers may want to try the recipes, but would sample the home remedies at their own risk. Too bad there's really no recipe for porridge!

PEASE PORRIDGE HOT

IN THE SUMMER OF 1850, when Elisha Marshall Pease came up to Connecticut from Texas to claim as his bride his distant cousin, Lucadia Christiana Niles, he was already an established lawyer in Brazoria, Texas. Living conditions in Brazoria, as in most Texas towns, were fairly primitive at this time. Household goods, food and medical supplies were hard to come by, so on the way to the new home the prudent, newly-married couple shopped for the necessities of life (and a few luxuries) in New Orleans and Galveston. Before setting out by steamer from New York, they had purchased for their table Prince Albert silver: *6 forks, 12 tablespoons, 18 teaspoons, 2 salt spoons, 1 mustard spoon, a silver plated cruet set, a silver cup, 3 fruit knives, butter knife, 2 napkin rings, 1 pair silver candlesticks, snuffer and tray.* A Galveston store furnished the fender, the tongs and shovel to outfit the fireplace which would provide heat during the Texas northers. The lengthy list of groceries, both staple and fancy, and supplies for the medicine chest, were ordered in New Orleans, to go by boat to Galveston, and then up the Brazos River to Brazoria.

Bought of **J.A.SAUTERS**
Dealer in Parlour Dining & Bedroom furniture, Carpeting Matting floor & Table Oil cloth China Glass & Crockery ware Britania Japan Tin Wood & Willow ware Window Ornaments Curtains Shades & Blinds Fancy Dry Goods Table & Bed Linnens, Cutllery Looking Glasses &. &.
Tremont Street Galveston

1 Iron Fender	5	00
1 Wire "	4	00
1 Set Brass Shovel tongs & Poker	7	00
1 " " top " "	2	50
1 pr Brass Hooks	2	25

Paymt Recd
J.A.Sauter.

$ 20. 75

Galveston 28 Novbr 50.
  2 Set Mosquito Rods   5 00
  3 " Rings   9 25
  1 pr Grape patten Candle Shades   35. 00

3

NEW ORLEANS, 7 ?abr. 18 50

Mrs. E. M. Pease   "Rancho"

Bought of H. L. STONE & CO.,

Importers & Wholesale Grocers, and Agents for the Hazard Powder Co.

Nos. 57 & 59 COMMON STREET.

Bill at Stone N. O. —

1 Bag Java Coffee	62 ℔ @ 15¢	9 30
2 Bbls Flour	@ 5½	11 00
1 Box Lf Sugar 203. 37 166	@ 1/	20 75
½ Bbl R Wheat		4 00
1 Bx Sp Candles 31	@ 4½	13 64
1 Can $1.00 5 Gals Sperm Oil	@ 10/	7 25
1 R Half Gall Pickles		5 50
1 Bbl S C Hams 268 234	@ 11	25 74
1 Box Cod Fish		90
½ Bbl No 1 Mackerel		3 50
1 Bx Ham Preserved		9 00
1 Bx Cayenne Pepper		1 50
5 ℔ Black Pepper	@ 10	50
2 " Ground Ginger	@ 1/	25
2 " Cloves	@ 40¢	80
1 Matt Cinnamon 2 3/4	@ 45¢	1 23
1 ℔ Nutmegs	@ 10/	1 25
3 ℔ 1 ℔ Cans Mustard	@ 4/	1 50
2 Bxs Fine Tea 6½	@ 12/	9 00
1 Bx Starch 37	@ 8	2 96
1 ℔ Indigo	@ 10/	1 25
1 Keg Cranberries	@ 3½	2 25
½ Bbl Lf Dried Apples 50 65	6	4 40
Carried Forward		137 47

Amount blo forwardf 137.49

2 Bags F Salt   .75
1 Bbl Cider Vinegar   3½   3.50
1 Bx Raisins   o   3.00
½ Bbl of Rice 127 117   5   6.35
20lb Currants   10   2.00
1 Bx Loaf   71   6   4.26
½ Dz Curre Candies   2   1.50
1 Demijohn 9¾ Gals Maglery 48   20.75
1   Do bj 5 Gals Port   2½   13.25
1   Do bj 5 Gals Modena 3½ 18.25
½ Bbl S M Beef   10.00
1 Bbl M S Pork   13.00
2 Pots Currie Ginger   31¾   3.50
1 No hlf Bx Sardines   4.50
1 Bx Chocolate   2.25
1 Bx Soda Biscuits   2.00
1 Dz Catsup Assorted   4.50
1 Keg Grapes   3.00
1 Basket Olive Oil   5.00
     Drayage & Marin Bont   1.25
                                  _____
                                  $259.38

Insurance to Brazoria
amn/285 p Marin S ke - 1s ???   4.99
                          Dray 2614 37
     Cash   ~   150
                          _____
          Ballance ~ 114 37

WHEN THE PEASES arrived in Brazoria, Lucadia soon found that housekeeping in her frame cottage was not just for two. Carrie Pease, Marshall's sister, accompanied the newlyweds to Brazoria to remain a year. In 1851, the first child, Carrie Augusta, was born. In 1852, the young family made their first trip back to Connecticut, and Juliet Niles, Lucadia's sister, came with them when they returned to Texas. The year 1853 saw the birth of another daughter, Julia Maria. Besides the family there were also always three or four slaves who served as house and yard servants, and who must be fed, clothed and cared for. In addition to the more or less permanent guests, visitors to Brazoria from outlying plantations were always welcomed for a night's visit and meals as desired. Inns were few and poorly kept, so reciprocal hospitality was expected, and received, from one's friends. When the court was held in Brazoria, Marshall Pease would bring his fellow lawyers home for dinner, or tea (supper). Or if there was a special occasion, such as a ball at the court house, or a revival, there were apt to be many guests. Cooking was in quantity, and Lucadia soon learned that, above all, Texans preferred meat, and the spicier the better.

To make spiced Beef

Select a fine fat round, weighing about 25 pounds. 3 ounces of Salt petre, 1 ounce of cloves, half an ounce of Allspice, 1 large nutmeg, and a quart of Salt, pound them all together very fine, take the bone out, rub it well with this mixture, on both sides, put some of it at the bottom of a tub just large enough to hold the beef, lay it in and strew the remainder on top, rub it well every day for 2 weeks, at the end of this time wash the beef, bind it with tape, fill the hole where the bone was, with a piece of fat, lay it in a pan of convenient size. Strew a little suet on the top, pour over it a pint of water, it will take five hours to bake.

IN HER EARLY ATTEMPTS at housekeeping Lucadia probably profited much from the visit of her older sister Juliet in 1852-53. Miss Niles was a typically thrifty, industrious New England spinster, who had scant respect for "shiftless Southerners." As the oldest of the four Niles girls, she was the most practical member of the family, and helped Lucadia train her colored servants and gave her various household hints. Although in later years Juliet made many visits to the gracious Pease family home, Woodlawn, in Austin, she never quite got over her first impressions of Texas, of the muddy streets in Brazoria and the generally primitive living conditions of the pioneer settlement. Before the day of detergents, she probably helped fight the Brazoria mud with homemade washing preparations.

Washing preparation

2 lbs soda Ash
1 lb unslacked lime
1 gallon water
boil 20 minutes.
Then add
2 gallons cold water and let it stand and settle. Then bottle — use 1 tea cup full to two pails water heat the water, then put the clothes in and boil them. Suds and rinse and they are nicely washed —

A letter of Juliet Niles, from Brazoria, January 5, 1853

....I shall go home as soon as I can in the spring. I hope as early as April if possible. We do not go out much & live as quiet as snails. That is I do. L has enough to busy herself superintending her housekeeping, which is no slight matter I assure you, ... the weather is delightful, but the mud is a great drawback on these pleasant days — & as I fear to get stuck beyond the power of extrication, & may be take root & grow in this boasted productive soil, a "consummation" not devoutly to be wished, I do not venture out much. We occasionally receive a genteel call from the ladies of the town...

THE PEASES bought a lot in Brazoria and made plans to build a home there. They planted a garden on the lot, and collected advice from their friends, such as how *to oil bricks before using instead of painting—(to exclude dampness)*. Wall paint was to be made by the following recipe:

Wall Paint

Take 8 ounces of freshly slacked lime and mix it in an earthen vessel with 3 quarts of skimmed milk (not sour): Then in another vessel mix three and a half pounds of Paris White with 3 pints of the Milk—When these mixtures are well stirred up, put them together and add six ounces of linseed oil. Mix them well and it will be ready for use and is considered by many equal to oil paint. It is excellent for walls and ceilings. Any shade may be made by the addition of dry pigments—

But the Brazoria home was never built, for Elisha Marshall Pease was elected Governor of Texas in 1853, and in December of that year the little family moved to Austin. There was no Governor's Mansion then, so the Peases roomed and boarded with Mrs. Susan Ward, the wife of Thomas William (or Peg Leg) Ward, who at that time was serving as the United States Consul at Panama. Lucadia was happy to be relieved for a while from the duties of housekeeping, and was pleased with the fare that Mrs. Ward provided.

Dear Sister,

We have a very good table more to my taste than any I have seen in Texas, and I often wish you were here at breakfast that you might disclaim what you used to say, that you had never seen a good beef steak in Texas, for I never ate anywhere better broiled & buttered steaks than we have daily, nor better light bread. Then we have mince pies and crullers and many northern dishes...I often ride in the carriage around the Town, and there are beautiful drives in every direction—The roads are excellent, rocky and hilly, but smooth and dry, and the scenery is very pretty. The new Capitol is a fine building built of stone found in this vicinity, whitish color, and admitting of a polish. They are building a very good Episcopal Church at present the churches are small, and finished with domestic, which is put on so neatly that they look quite well. There are a few good blocks of stores on the principal street, and when told that it is only eight or ten years since the Indians came into the center of the Town and in the daytime took off several children...one is more surprized at the improvements they see here, than that, they are no greater.

Your Aff.
Lu

11

THE PEASE SLAVES had come to Austin with their master, and the yard servant Tom was soon put to work making a garden on Mrs. Ward's property. Lucadia wrote: "We have sweet corn from seed I brought from home, and an abundance of the common garden vegetables." But she wished she could exchange the supply of tomatoes "for some of your more desirable eatables." Her freedom from housekeeping allowed Lucadia to take drives in the hills around Austin, and she became acquainted with the Austin ladies, whom she found "very agreeable and friendly."

Lucadia particularly enjoyed her association with Mrs. Ward, and felt genuine regret when Mrs. Ward decided that she must move north to be nearer her family. Governor Pease decided to continue renting the Ward house, and bought some of Mrs. Ward's household effects to add to the small store of furniture and equipment that it had seemed worthwhile to transport overland from Brazoria.

Gov. Pease

Bot of Mr. Ward

1	Looking Glass		3.25
1	Skillton	64	75
3	Iwps 1 of 6 flat Irons &c 1.00		2.75
1	Beauro 25f 1 Carpet 41f		66.00
2	Bed Comforts 2.25 1.50		3.75
1	" Do 1.85		1.85
1	Pr Blankets		4.61
5	Pickle Dishes	1/	62
2	Large Dishes	1.55	3.10
1	Straw Cutter		8.00
1	Steel Mill		1.50
4	Tubs &c		2.40
1	Grinde Stone		3.12
1	Wheel Barrow		2.00
1	Bathing Tub		8.00
1	Meat Saw		1.00
			114.69
	Deduct Carpet & Beauro		66.00
			46.69
1	Wool Mattrass		15.00
1	Shovel & tongs in Kitchen		1.25
			62.94

Recd payment 3 May 1854

Thomas Wm Ward
By Susson D Ward

WHILE LUCADIA was enjoying her new life in Austin, taking rides into the hills, and admiring the wild flowers on the prairie, poor sister Juliet Niles, away off in Poquonock, Connecticut, was miserable. Besides a set of bad impressions, she had acquired in Texas the "chills and fever." Despite Marshall's duties as governor, he had time to continue as family physician and prescribe for his sister-in-law, through Lucadia's letter.

... I will write you what Marshall says you must do if you wish to be cured entirely of the chills and fever — and you must follow his directions implicitly. He wishes you were here where he is sure you would soon be well. Firstly, wear flannel next the skin — if the bowels are not open, take a dose of castor oil, two tablespoonsfulls about the right quantity. The day the fever is on, refrain entirely from eating, drink freely to quench thirst — tea, warm or cold whichever is preferable, without milk or sugar — as soon as the fever leaves, take two grains of quinine in half a wine glass of Madeira wine, or about a half a tablespoonfull of French brandy, repeat the dose in two hours unless it makes your head ache very much, in which case, wait three hours before repeating it — take a third and fourth dose after the same interval of time, not eating anything for at least one hour after taking it, or one hour before taking it — if this treatment does not prevent the fever from returning, then after each return of the fever pursue the same course until the fever does stop. After the fever has ceased to return take one dose every morning for at least three weeks — avoid eating milk or hearty food, such as butter, meats and gravies, take these doses in the morning before eating, and do not eat for at least an hour after taking it ...

14

To Juliet:

Austin City. Feby 9th /54 —

My dear Sister,

I received a letter from Maria to day who tells me you had had a chill, and been so very sick as to consent to consult a Doctor — I am very much distressed to learn that you have again suffered with chills, attributable I suppose to your having visited Texas, and am writing you at once, with the hope that you will follow Marshalls prescriptions, who feels very confident if you will do so, you will escape a return of the disease —

I like Austin very much, it is very hilly, and more like New England than any other place I have seen in Texas — There are so many pleasant drives, in every direction that I keep big Sam and the horses and carriage in daily use, taking with me some acquaintance or the children to drive — Marshall has been very much engaged since we have been here, but the Legislature will adjourn in a few days when he expects to be at leisure and, after a few weeks we intend making a trip to San Antonia, a town of more interest (having been an old settlement of the Spaniards), than any in the State — You would enjoy visiting us here I think much better than at Marguine, the Country is so beautiful and then there is so much society — and the ladies with whom I have become acquainted are very agreeable and friendly —

15

ANOTHER LITTLE DAUGHTER, Anne Marshall, was born in 1854, and now the question of the health of their children took precedence over any other concern. Austin was considered more healthful than Brazoria, and physicians were more numerous. The newspapers of the day printed frequent announcements for the doctors, who extolled their skill, much as the merchants advertised their goods.

Names of dread diseases like "cholera infantum" were some times applied to childhood ailments that were less frightening than the words connoted, although the prescription sounds awesome enough.

Prescription for Cholera

'Cholera Infantum' &c &c
  Take 1/3 Oz Spts Camphor
      1/3 do Laudanum
      1/3 do Gum Catechire dissolved
Directions
  Shake them well together and
    To a person 10 years give 5 drops
    "   "   "   20 "   "10 to 20"
    "   "   "   30 "   "25 " 40"
    "   " " 40 or 50" "40 " 50"
  Once or twice a day until relieved
                              Benj Owen Payn
Austin
    July 11th 1855

Generally the little Pease girls were merry, vigorous children whose health was guarded by common sense and wise parental guidance, not by the treatment of such as Doctor Ogden.

DOCTOR J. M. OGDEN,

Office 710 Congress Avenue, over Potosky's Cigar Store.

A GRADUATE OF THE UNIVERSITY OF DUBLIN.

HAVING been for years a Student at the large Hospitals of Dublin and New-York, and through a large and varied practice during fifteen years, has gained the most thorough knowledge of the nature of all diseases and the treatment thereof. These things being so, he has had in his extensive practice the most unbounded success; very often effecting cures where every known remedy had been tried and all hope of restoration to health had been despaired of.

Nobody who suffered from that life-embittering and tedious disease—dyspepsia—has ever in vain called upon Dr. OGDEN. In every case has he, by his new method of treatment, restored the functions of the stomach, and with it the health and vigor of the patient.

For his treatment of LADIES' DISEASES, Dr. OGDEN is deservedly celebrated, and no lady suffering from any of the diseases peculiar to the female system should fail to call on him, as they will thereby be quickly relieved, and ultimately restored to health.

"Diseases of a Private Nature"

Dr. OGDEN has made a specialty, and this scourge of humanity, unsuccessfully treated by most physicians, is easily and quickly overcome by his new treatment. Dr. OGDEN will always guarantee a cure in any case of Syphilitic disease which may come under his treatment, and hundreds of persons can testify that in cases of a Syphilitic nature, where other physicians have failed, Dr. OGDEN has always been successful.

Nervous Debility, Seminal Weakness, Impotency, et., etc., either caused by abuse, quickly and permanently relieved, and full power restored. No man is too old, and no young man too debilitated, to be completely reinvigorated and rejuvenated by the treatment of Dr. OGDEN.

☞ Dr. OGDEN wishes to call attention to his New Discovery, by which he can, by the help of the Microscope and Chemistry, discover if there is any Syphilitic Poison in the blood; which is of the greatest importance, as persons having had Venereal Diseases often believe themselves cured, while the poison still remains in the blood, to break out sooner or later.

Dr. Ogden has located in Austin. Office 710 Congress Avenue, over Potosky's Cigar and Tobacco Store.

☞ *Consultations strictly confidential.* ☜

Austin Evening News Print.

17

A RESIDENCE for the Governor of Texas was in the process of construction during Governor Pease's first term.

Completion was scheduled for January of 1856, but there were numerous delays. It was Lucadia's year to go north, to see her family, but she put off her trip until late in May, hoping to superintend the great move. By the middle of June, when the Mansion was finally ready, she and her children had left, and to Marshall fell the task of moving their possessions into their new home. Letters went back and forth, full of the details of where the furniture was placed and so on. Then in August, Governor Pease felt well enough settled to submit the Mansion to public inspection. He had printed and circulated to the Legislature and to all the citizens of Austin an invitation to the first party to be given by the Chief Executive for the people.

The affair was a great success. Dutch John, proprietor of a local restaurant, prepared the food, and Lucadia's lady friends assisted the Governor in entertaining the more than 500 guests who came. Proof that "the table was the finest I ever saw set in Austin" is the size of the bill the Governor had to pay to L. Malitzky and the detailed description he wrote to Lucadia.

Governor Pease   Austin 2/9 '56
       to L Malitzkys

Aug 23.	Six Turkeys	$ 15	00
	Six Ducks	6	00
	two Doz. Chickens	15	00
	two Shoats	10	00
	forthy Loaves of Bread	4	00
	five pound of butter	1	50
	Coffee & tea	12	00
	Cakes ———	35	00
	ten pound of Candy	5	00
	ten pound of Almonds	4	00
		$107	50
	for brocken Crockery	$ 8	30
	for carpenter work	3	00
	for hauling	3	00
		$121	80

Received Payment in full.
     L W Holzinger
     for L Malitzky

...Last night my great party came off, and Mr. Purvis says it is the talk about Town that it was the best one ever got up in Austin. The Ladies turned out well. There was a perfect jam, it is estimated that there were present at different times during the evening at least five hundred persons; and that over three hundred staid to the supper. The table was the finest I ever saw set in Austin—There was no lack of material of every kind, and everything was arranged with the best taste, for which I am indebted to Mrs. Sam Harris, Mrs. Jack Harris and Mrs. Bullard of Matagorda. I was quite unwell all day Saturday until dark. In the evening I felt much better and tried to make myself as agreeable as possible, but did not taste the supper. I feel relieved now it is over. I knew it was expected of me, as the first occupant of the new Executive Mansion—It was the first Public party ever given by a Governor of Texas, and I felt anxious that it should be a creditable one, as it will be the standard by which others to be given by my successors will be measured. The result has satisfied me, and I believe my friends were proud of it—My only regret about it is that you could not have been here to enjoy it, and divide with me the responsibility. Though absent your labors contributed greatly to the excellence of the supper, for all the brandied fruit and most of the preserves were of your making.

20

Austin 24th Aug" 56
Sunday night

My Dear Wife

Your excellent letter of the 7th inst was
received this afternoon, and relieved my anxiety,
which had become very intense about you, as
your previous letter was dated the 25th of July,
Tell our darlings, Pappa is very happy to learn
that they have been good and he will love
them more than ever, he hopes Carrie will be able to
read when she comes home, and if she is, he
will have a nice present for her, he hopes
Julie has not forgot her knowledge of geography,
and that Anna will talk quite well when he meets
them, they shall all have nice presents when they come,
I am grateful that you had so pleasant
a visit at Berlin and Newburn, You were particularly fortunate in meeting your Rochester and
Troy friends,   In regard to the Carriage use your
own judgment, about the style and price and I
shall be satisfied, do not let it be too heavy or large,
for you know our roads are heavy, Let them know
it is for use at the South and they will know the
width of the truck it should make — Emily says
she uses the cold bath regularly & she is much better,
I feel no desire for the apples you write about, but
I should enjoy the Suckatash much, vegetables of every
kind have become uncommonly scarce this summer,

21

Even WHEN LUCADIA was relaxing from her housekeeping duties while visiting her mother and sisters in Connecticut, she prudently thought of the winter ahead. She helped to gather apples from the Niles trees, and dried them for pies to be made in Austin. One misadventure resulting from her foresightedness upset her greatly. She packed some home grown, home canned vegetables in her trunk, and weeks later, when she opened her trunk in Austin, she found a can of sweet corn had exploded in transit and ruined several of her best dresses. Marshall offered to replace the dresses, but she was inconsolable!

When Lucadia and the children returned in the fall of 1856 to their new home, she was busier than ever with her homemaking duties in the beautiful new Governor's Mansion. Under her direction a garden was planted and hogs from the Executive pig pen were slaughtered.

My dear Sister,

Your letter containing my fringe was duly received, and although I had not missed it, still it was very acceptable. I have had no occasion yet to wear the dress and have not had it made. I made me a basque of the black broadcloth, which I bought. And find it a very useful and comfortable article of dress. The figured black silk which I wear with it looks almost as well as new, and although I wear it every day at home, I do not anticipate it will ever wear out— ...And the seeds were very acceptable. Have planted peas Irish Potatoes & most of the early vegetables—You know we have no very decided seasons here, one day will be very windy and cold, and the next quite summer like....we have had no rain here this winter, and the ground is so dry I fear I shall not succeed in making flowers grow very well...We have just killed six hogs and I am deep in the business of lard making and curing of hams. We shall put up twelve hogs this winter and hope to have enough—last year they had to buy pork while I was away—

Aff—
Lu

THE PEASES entertained more guests than ever, and when two young ladies visited them at the Mansion, Lucadia gave a party for seventy in their honor. Tableaux were the entertainment, and Lucadia prepared elegant refreshments. *I made cake and Emily cooked hams and turkeys, but as my fruit cake was quite new and very rich I decided to not use it, but had the confectioners make me two large pyramid loafs, and with chicken and lobster salad, and custard and jellies &c &c the two long tables looked very handsomely—Then I began to think about my dress, and decided to wear the silk you bought for me at N. York, and by putting the short basque under the skirt and by the use of a profusion of ribbons, I dressed myself quite to my satisfaction. The tableaux went off with great eclat, many of the guests had never seen any before, one scene was a wedding scene Miss Groce with a bridal wreath and veil, and Mr. Fisher as groom. Mr. Robards with his bands on, and prayer book in hand, and Marshall giving away the bride—made a very pretty picture—Then they sent for me to take a part in the scene of 'Moses' in the Vicar of Wakefield 'proposing to go to the fair'—and I put my calico wrapper over my dress, and made I suppose a very good wife for the vicar—Then we had dancing which lasted till a late or rather early hour—*

Austin, April 10th/37.

My dear Augusta,

I was quite delighted last night to receive a letter from you. We have none of us I think been very prompt correspondents of late — All your items of news were news indeed to me. I had no intimation or suspicion that our nephew or nephews was in expectancy, but shall be ready to offer my congratulations upon the first intimation of the event.

I have been very much occupied in having company, and visiting for three or four weeks past — Mr Grace, Mrs Whartons brother wrote to Marshall and Mr Harris that his daughter and a cousin of hers Miss Williams were on the point of visiting Austin and their politeness and attention to the ladies was requested

AT THE END of Governor Pease's second term, in December 1857, the family moved from the Mansion. For a year they rented the James H. Raymond house, which resembled the Mansion and had also been built by Abner Cook. Soon after coming to Austin, Marshall Pease had bought property to the west of Austin, and Lucadia's letters often mentioned their intention of building their own home. Instead, in 1859, the Peases purchased another Abner Cook house, that of James B. Shaw. Their beautiful home, on the gentle hills above Shoal Creek, they named, after much thought, Wood Lawn (now written as one word). While Marshall re-established his law practice, Lucadia was busy making a happy home for her husband and their three children. Although now almost in the center of Austin, Woodlawn was then considered a country residence. Visitors came not just for a meal, but for overnight, or for weeks at a time. The hospitality that was to be the hallmark of Woodlawn from then on was first started by Lucadia at this time, and she probably collected recipes as we do today.

Sponge Cake

2 cupsfull powdered sugar

2 cupfuls flour sifted —

2 tea spoonsfuls baking powders —

4 eggs —

3/4 teacup boiling water —

A pinch of salt —

Lemon to taste —

Beat the whites and yolks of
the eggs separately — Add
the boiling water
After all the other
ingredients have been
mixed and bake in a moderate
oven —

Divinity Candy.

1st Part.

To one half cup of sugar, add
enough water to dissolve, and cook
until when dropped from a spoon,
it spins a good thread. Beat this
into the well beaten whites of three
eggs. (Before beating the whites of the
eggs, a pinch of salt should be add.)

2nd. Part.

To three cups of sugar and one
cup of corn syrup add one cup
of water and boil until when
dropped in cold water it becomes
quite hard. Stir this into the
first mixture, add one or two cups
of pecans and beat well. Then
pour it on a buttered platter and

let cool before cutting.

"Karo Corn Syrup" gives the candy
a more delicate flavor than any
of the other syrups.

EXTENSIVE ACREAGE surrounded the stately home, and the presence of wild grape vines probably started Lucadia to experimenting with the possibility of making mustang wine. Recipes for wine-making seem to have been collected by Sophie R. Fisher, a relative of the Harris family, who were perhaps the Peases' oldest Texas friends. Mr. Carrington's recipe seems simpler, but the Peases probably preferred Judge Townes' method, as the Towneses were old Brazoria neighbors who also moved early to Austin.

— Mr. Carrington's Receipt —

Carefully pick the grapes from stem — throwing away such as are not ripe, also such as are decayed — Then wash them — Wash the grapes & put them in a clean barrell, allowing to each gallon of the grapes, one gallon of pure water — Put the barrell in a cool place & let it stand for three or four days — When fermentation ceases the seed & hulls of grapes ascend to the top — Draw off & carefully strain — Then add 3 lbs sugar to the gallon & let it remain 8 or 10 days & it is ready for use — You may then bottle it, & it will grow better as it increases in age.

White wine is made precisely as the above, omitting the outside hull of the grape —

Much the most simple way of making wine & the best — SRF.

Mr Carrington's Receipt –

Carefully pick the Grapes from stem – Throwing
away such as are not ripe, also such as are
decayed – Then wash them –
Mash the grapes & put them in a clean barrell,
allowing to each gallon of the grapes, one
gallon of Pure Water – Put the barrell in
a cool place & let it stand for, three or four
days – When fermentation ceases the seed
& hulls of grapes ascend to the top – Draw
off & carefully strain – Then add 3 lbs Sugar
to the gallon & let it remain 8 or 10 days, &
it is ready for use – You may then bottle
it, & it will grow better as it increases in age.

White Wine is made precisely as the above,
omitting the out side hull of the grape –

SOON THE HAPPY FAMILY LIFE was saddened by the coming of the Civil War and the death of the youngest daughter. Lucadia and Marshall kept on, making as good a home as possible. Housekeeping continued, but ingenuity was more necessary than money.

Aug. 30/65

You would be amused to know to what expedients we resorted during the years of the Confederacy to supply ourselves with the many necessaries which the blockade deprived us of. This ink first occurs to me, which is a homemade manufacture and which, its the only kind we have had since the war, is made of sumac berries boiled and strained—The bonnets and hats for men and women have all been home made, some of corn shucks or husks or rye or wheat straw bleached split grain—then our gloves, if we had any, were spun, knit, colored, and all done by ourselves, in shoemaking I became quite adept particularly in the art of cobbling— We made our own soda, much of our toilet soap, and in all the different varieties of tallow candles I most particularly prided myself that I excelled my neighbor, the prickly pear hardening, alum clarifying, small twisted wicks, were all topics of conversation with visitors. But coloring was the great art of arts, the leaves, berries, bark and roots of every tree was tried, the long moss, short moss simmered and boiled, and if the color did not equal the gorgeousness of Syrian dyes, satisfied us with their variety—And when we called upon our friends, instead of discussing the merits of the last published novel, we talked of some practical matter of economy—If sometimes when we expected a yellow or grey color, it came from the dye green or brown, we had only to try again with the hope of better luck—In the article of starch too, we experimented largely—starch made of green corn, wheat starch, flour starch, bran starch all were tried, with various success. Then I had all the sewing for my family, including mending, and you can understand I had not many idle moments.

Wood Lawn Aug 30/65—

My dear Sister,

I have not received a letter from you, since the one Mrs Swanson sent me written last April. Neither have I written you for a long time, for various reasons, one of which is, we have no mails beyond Texas. Another is, that I hoped every week that some means would offer that we could go North. Some of our friends here, have avoided the quarantine regulations, by the aid of U.S. transports and I now very much regret that we did not avail ourselves of the kindness of a Fed' from here, who offered to escort us and who wrote us that he had a quick and safe journey to New Orleans, the most dreaded part of the journey—We have now the fear of yellow fever which it is rumored

As SOON as it was possible after peace came, the Pease family went north to visit their relatives. Carrie and Julia were now of an age to need systematic schooling. Schools in Texas were disorganized, and so for several years Lucadia and the girls remained in Connecticut so that the children might have educational advantages that both parents thought so necessary. Marshall went back to Texas to look after his property and start up his law practice again. When Marshall was appointed Military Governor of Texas in 1867, Lucadia left the girls in school, under the care of her sisters, and came to Austin. The Peases boarded in town with friends, for they did not wish to live in the Governor's Mansion again, and had not the heart to reopen Woodlawn without the girls and with inadequate help. By 1870, the Pease family was back at their beloved Woodlawn, except for Julia, who entered Vassar College in the fall of 1870, from which she was graduated in 1875. A menu of Thanksgiving dinner at Vassar in 1872 shows that college girls of that day were not as worried about their caloric intake as those of today.

Vassar College.

Thanksgiving Dinner.

Nov. 28th, 1872.

BILL OF FARE.

SOUP.

Oyster. Mock Turtle.

BOILED.

Salmon—Anchovy Sauce. Turkey—Oyster Sauce.

ROAST.

Beef. Chicken. Lamb.

Turkey—Cranberry Sauce.

Goose—Apple Sauce.

COLD ORNAMENTAL DISHES.

Chicken Salad. Boned Turkey. Lobster Salad.

Tongue. Jelly. Ham.

ENTREE.

Poularde a la Marengo.

Oyster Vol-au-vent. Duck salni-aux-Olives.

Filet d'alyan braise aux Champignons.

VEGETABLES.

Mashed Potatoes. Green Peas.

Sweet Corn. Tomatoes. Sweet Potatoes.

RELISHES.

Mixed Pickles. Celery. Chow Chow.

Beets. Worcestershire Sauce. Olives.

PASTRY.

Cheese.

Cranberry Tart Pie. Mince Pie. Hubbard Squash Pie.

Jelly Tarts. Silver, Gold and Fruit Cake. Lemon Jelly.

Lady Fingers.

DESSERT.

Havana Oranges. Figs. Raisins. Assorted Nuts.

Catawba, Isabella and Malaga Grapes.

Beurre D'Anjou. Beurre Bosc.

Vanilla and Chocolate Ice Cream.

TEA. COFFEE.

ALTHOUGH THE GIRLS were nearly grown, the parents continued to watch over their health and worry especially about Julia, who was so far away. Lucadia feared continually that Julia might strain her eyes from over-use while studying, and cautioned her not to waste her precious eyesight on fancy work. The Peases were probably too knowledgable to put much faith in Doctor Duvall's advice.

It is doubtful also whether the recipe for cleaning teeth was the one recommended by the parents for their young daughters.

Gum guaiacum and orris root of each one ounce. Camphor gum a teaspoonful, put then in a pint of good Brandy, let the mixture infirm ten days and filter the liquid gradually through a cloth into a suitable vessel. Wash and clense the teeth once in 24 hours.

The Eyesight

To preserve it for life, and to restore impaired vision —
also to have bright and sparkling eyes —

Let there be an occasional pressure of the finger on
the ball of the eyes. And let the pressure always be
from the nose and toward the temples, and wash the
eyes three times a day in a gallon of cold water (mixture of) in which there has been previously dissolved
a quarter of an ounce of Cream of Tartar and two ounces
of refined Sugar. If this simple advice is followed, the
day is not distant when partial blindness shall dis-
appear from the world. I do not wish to practice deceit
in this book therefore people must not understand me
to say that this will give sight to those who are blind:
but several cases of blindness from birth, Have been
cured by it. And I do say that very great help, and no
hurt may be obtained in all cases. Nearly twenty years
ago, being then in this country, I imparted this simple
remedy to the venerable John Q. Adams, who by its
use preserved his eyesight till death. If the foregoing
remarks are strictly observed with frequent ablutions,
they will prove of incalcuable advantage to the people.

DOCTOR E. DUVALL

CARRIE HERSELF became a housewife in January of 1875, when she was married in the parlor at Woodlawn. She and her husband George Graham lived with her family for a time after her marriage, and she took over much of the housekeeping. She was particularly successful with cakes and pies, such as

Mock Mince Pie

5 crackers
2 Eggs
2 2/3 cups of boiling water
1 cup Sugar
1 cup Molasses
½ cup Butter
½ cup Vinegar
1 teaspoonful of each kind of spice
   Cloves Cinnamon & Allspice
   Raisins & Currants
Roll the crackers and mix all the ingredients together with the water, except the eggs. Beat the eggs well and add them to the rest when it is cool. Cut the raisins and add them just before covering the jar.

Cake :

Whites of 4 eggs -
2 cups sugar -
1/2 " butter -
1/2 " milk & water
1 1/2 flour (cups)

mix butter & sugar lightly
add whites of eggs without
beating - add milk
and flour with baking-
powder - flour with
vanilla - beat altogether
ten minutes -

SOON THERE WERE GRANDCHILDREN at Wood-lawn, and Grandmother Lucadia, Aunt Julia (now home for good from Vassar) as well as the young mother Carrie tried their hand at cooking wholesome goodies, such as:

Queen of Puddings

1 pint of nice bread crumbs
1 quart of milk
Yolk of four eggs
Grated rind of 1 lemon
Piece of butter size of egg
Bake like custard
When baked spread over the top slices of jelly, and cover the whole with the whites of eggs beaten to a stiff froth, with one cup of sugar, and the juice of the lemon. Brown lightly—

Because of her children, Carrie could not accompany the Peases to the Philadelphia Centennial World's Fair in 1876, but she doubtless read eagerly all the enticing literature that they brought home—the leaflets advertising such great advancement in housekeeping as cooked meats in cans, baking powder, dried eggs—and revolutionary new laborsaving equipment, like the oscillating churn.

Buxom little dairy-maid,
Belle of all the butter trade:
In the twinkling of an eye,
You can make the butter fly;
When the butter-milk comes up,
Fill it in a butter-cup,
And I'll pledge you in a bumper,
For you are a " real thumper!"

McLOUGHLIN BROS. Manuf. N. Y.

41

BULLARD'S
Oscillating Churn.

MANUFACTURED BY

BULLARD & ELLSWORTH,

BARRE, MASSACHUSETTS.

To the Dairymen of the World:

We offer the Oscillating Churn to the public solely upon its merits, and we do this with the utmost confidence in its ability to satisfy a long existing want, and secure the approval of all who try it. We claim in the oscillating churn to have discovered the most thorough and common sense application of the only correct principle in churning, and consequently claim it to be the most perfect churn now in use. In proof of this, we would respectfully call your attention to the opinions of the following prominent dairymen who use it.

Col. GEORGE E. WARING, Jr., of the American Agriculturist.

"I have never seen a churn for which I would exchange it."

A. W. CHEEVER, of the New England Farmer.

"There is almost no waste of cream, and the ease with which it works has lessened the dread of churning day one-half."

Prof. L. B. ARNOLD, Secretary of the American Dairyman's Association.

Thinks "the work done better than in the dash churn."

Hon. HARRIS LEWIS, Treasurer of the American Dairyman's Association.

"It is the best churn I ever used, and I like it better and better the more I use it."

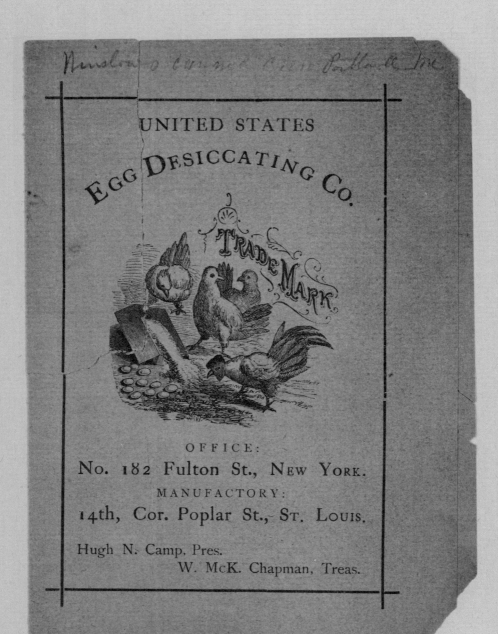

Wilson Packing Company,

CHICAGO, ILL.,

PACKERS OF THEIR CELEBRATED

COOKED MEATS

IN HERMETICALLY SEALED CANS,

READY FOR THE TABLE.

PATENTED MARCH 30th. 1874.

Indorsed by the most prominent Scientists of the Country, and in general use on Land and Sea in all parts of the World.

We have invested over half a million dollars in our business, and having our reputation and integrity to sustain, issue this circular to the public, that the consumer may, with perfect confidence, rely upon our assurance of the PERFECT PURITY of our meats, as WE USE NO CHEMICALS WHATEVER IN THEIR PREPARATION.

It is a well-known and creditable fact that Chicago has the most stringent sanitary inspection of Cattle for slaughtering of any city in the Union.

All cattle used by us are purchased at the great Chicago "Live Stock" market, and all our packing is done *in* Chicago.

These goods have now been in general use for nearly *Three Years*, and have won the highest *encomiums* from the *Medical Faculty*, the *Trade* and the *Consumer*, for their *superiority* over any other Preserved Meats on the market, and for their NUTRITIOUS, WHOLESOME and ECONOMICAL qualities.

ONLY THE BEST GRADES OF MEATS ARE USED, and the greatest care and skill exercised in curing and canning, and the consumption of these justly famous goods has been so large, (aggregating millions of cans,) that the entire facilities of our immense Packing Houses in Chicago have not been equal, at times, to supply the demand, though we take special pride in announcing that we have this year erected additional works, thereby doubling our previous capacity, and we now have the LARGEST BEEF PACKING ESTABLISHMENT IN THE UNITED STATES, and are thus enabled to supply the demand, however great.

IN 1879, GOVERNOR PEASE accepted appointment as Collector of Customs at Galveston. In the year or so that he remained there, Lucadia did little housekeeping, for she and Marshall lived at the Tremont Hotel. Carrie and the children visited them occasionally, but the young Grahams had the responsibility of keeping life at Woodlawn going. Julia was with her parents much of the time and became a belle in the gay Galveston society, as she was in less sophisticated Austin. No matter how frivolous her social life was, Julia had always the common sense and thriftiness of her New England parents. Even after dancing till the "wee sma' hours," she probably arose early the next morning and cleansed her ribbons by Mrs. Maxey's "receipt."

One quart of gasolene put in a preserve jar. put some pieces of old white domestic at the bottom. then fold your ribbons nicely and put in the jar. let them remain all night. morning shake them out and dry. nothing more and they look like new.

Mrs Marcy's receipt

JULIA AND LUCADIA both loved the ocean, and it is easy to imagine them walking along the beach collecting sea shells, and then polishing them.

Polishing shells &c

In general it happens when shells become dry they lose their natural, & fine luster—This may be easily restored by washing with clean water in which a little gum arabic has been dissolved. There are some, however which appear exceedingly dull upon the outer surface on account of the epidermis with which they are covered. This may be removed by steeping the shell in warm water & then rubbing hard with a brush. When the epidermis is thick it will be found necessary to mingle a little nitric acid with the water; this, however must be used with great caution since it destroys the luster of every part it touches & the water should only be impregnated sufficiently to remove the thick skin, without acting upon the shell beneath. The new skin must now be polished with chamois skin & finally with pulverized chalk. When these are ineffectual, pumice stone must be applied to rub off the coarse external layers & disclose the hidden beauties beneath.

Polishing Shells &c —

In general it happens when
shells become dry they lose
their natural & fine lustre.
This may be easily restored
by washing with clean water
in which a little gum arabic
has been dissolved. There are
some, however, which appear
exceedingly dull upon the
outer surface, on account of
the epidermis with which
they are covered. This may
be removed by steeping the
shell in warm water & then
rubbing hard with a brush.
when the epidermis is thick
it will be found necessary
to mingle a little nitric acid
with the water; this, however

49

THE GALVESTON INTERLUDE did not last long and once again the family was back in Austin. Carrie and George moved their little family into their own home. For a few years life went on as usual at Woodlawn, and then tragedy struck this loving family. Within the space of one year, Governor Pease and his eldest daughter Carrie were dead. Mrs. Pease was desolate and in desperate need of Julia's comforting attention. The young aunt had to be a substitute mother, caring for and cherishing Carrie's three remaining children, one a new born baby. Julia's carefree, social days were over, but she faced her new responsibilities with stout courage and loving intelligence. The years went by — some at Woodlawn, some in the East, with the Connecticut relatives or in New York, near the boarding schools of the growing Graham children. Then, as the end of the 19th century approached, Woodlawn once again became the prime example of gracious Austin hospitality. Age did not prevent Lucadia's interest in the developing complexities of life in Austin, as it changed from small town to city. Old friends were cherished and new ones made. The artist Elisabet Ney considered Woodlawn her second home.

Distinguished visitors were entertained as a matter of course at Woodlawn, and Julia must have always been on the look out for new recipes.

Milk Punch

One glass sweet milk
Two Teaspoonfulls pulverized sugar,
One Tablespoonfull Burbon Whiskey,
One Tablespoonfull Jamaica Rum,

   Put in shaker with crushed
ice and shake well.

Cooked
Mayonnaise dressing
1 tablespoon Mustard
1 " Sugar
3 " Olive Oil
A dash of cayenne
Mix throughly – add 3
eggs, one at a time –
1 cup of vinegar, a little
at a time – then 1 cup
of Milk in same way –
Cook until about as
thick as cream in
double boiler –
stirring occasionally
Oct 18th   M. E. Ladd

52

Wilhelm Busch — author

Comische Gedichte

Salad dressing —

pint of cream whipped
+ about 1/2 bottle of
(pint) of Durkees Salad
dressing —

Miss Margaret Runge —

Salad — Chopped eggs (seperatly)
1 egg to each person — grated
cheese, with Mayonaise viar —
All in a lettuce leaf —

IN ADDITION TO HER DUTIES to her family and as housekeeper for Woodlawn, Julia became one of the moving spirits in every venture that added to the cultural and social life of her city and state. On the practical side she was always ready to provide cakes for a church bazaar, to lend her home and her help to any group of people, young or old, who called on her for assistance. She loved the good old-fashioned food like corn pones:

Corn Pones

1 cupfull corn meal
¾   " flour
2 heaping teaspoon baking powder
1 egg
little salt
1 cupful milk
water sufficient to make batter—
Beat well—
Drop into hot fat and brown—

But one can imagine the fun she had, helping the young gentlemen of the Saturday Night Whist Club plan a really fancy party for their midwinter affair.

AFTER THE DEATH of Mrs. Pease in 1905, Miss Julia, as she was known to hundreds of Austin and Texas friends, continued to carry on the high tradition of Pease housekeeping. She herself did not die until 1918, so doubtless she coped with the meatless days of World War I and found ways to make appetizing desserts without sugar. The next generation of the family followed in her footsteps so that the very name of Woodlawn remained synonymous with the best of Texas hospitality.

· WOODLAWN · HOUSE · 1853 ·

PEASE PORRIDGE HOT *has been published con mucho gusto by The Encino Press for the Friends of the Austin Public Library. The text has been set by the Typographers in W. A. Dwiggins' Caledonia type, printed by Carlos Urtardo at the Whitley Company on Linweave Text paper supplied by the Lone Star Paper Company & bound by Custom Bookbinders, all according to the design by William D. Wittliff.*

EAGLE GAIL BORDEN BRAND

TIPPECANOE.

TRADE MARK. SAFE KIDNEY & LIVER CURE. WARNER'S SAFE RHEUMATIC CURE H.H.WARNER&CO. ROCHESTER N.Y.U.S.A. SAFE NERVINE. (SAFE PILLS.

SAFE DIABETES CURE.

STEEL